ANSWER KEY LONGMAN VISTA CLASS-7 SST

NCERT PATTERN BOOK. SOLUTION FROM BOOK ONLY.

SAREETAM BUDHOLIYA

Made with ♥ on the Notion Press Platform
www.notionpress.com

Contents

INDIA IN THE MEDIEVAL PERIOD

Chapter 1 - India In Medieval Period

Q1. Fill in the blanks:-

1. The early medieval period saw the emergence of **Palas, Rashtrakutas, Cholas**
2. The Persian wheel is related **to irrigation**.
3. The late medieval period spans between **13th to 18th century**
4. Al-Biruni come to India with Mahmud **of Ghazni.**

Q2. Match the following

Tarikh-ai-hind == Al-Biruni

Prithviraj Raso == Chand bardai

Sur Sagar ==Surdas

Ain-I-Akbari == Abul fazl

Padmawat == Malik Mohhamad Jayasi

Q3. State T/F?

1. The ruler in the sultanate and Mughal period called their Indian dominion Bharat. == **F**
2. Al-Masudi was an Arab traveler who traveled to India around the eighth century. == **T**
3. Domingo Paes was a French traveler who visited the court of Krishnadeva Raya of the Vijayanagr Empire. == **F**

4. Prithviraj Chauhan an Indian ruler from the chahamana Dynasty defeated Mohammad Ghori in a fierce battle. == **T**
5. The idea of Bhakti emerged during the ancient period around 500 BCE and its popularity declined in the medieval period. == **F**

Q4.1. Name some literary sources of the medieval period?

Ans Literary sources of the medieval period include manuscripts; "stories, poems, biographies" of different rulers and folk tales that have passed from generation to generation.biographies" of different rulers and folk tales that have passed from generation to generation.

Q4.2 Name three foreign traveler who visited India during the medieval period?

Ans.

1. Al-Masudi = 957 A.D. =Al-Masudi was An Arab traveller. In his book Muruj-ul-Zehab he has explained his journey.

2. Alberuni/Abu al-Rayhan Muhammad ibn Ahmad al-Biruni = 1024 A.D. – 1030 A.D.) = He was a Persian scholar. He accompanied Mahmud of Ghazni and wrote a book titled 'Tahqiq-i-hind'. He is considered the father of Indology.

3. Ibn Battuta = 1333 A.D. – 1347 A.D. = He was a Moroccan traveller. He visited India during the rule of Mohammed Bin Tughlaq. Rihla is a book written by Ibn Batuta.

Q4.3 Give two examples of archaeological sources from medieval period?

Ans. Coins related to this period, monuments and paiting.

Q4.4 What was the new invention used for irrigation called?

Ans. Persian Wheel.

Q4.5 Who wrote Akbarnama?

Ans. Abul fazal

Q5.1 What are Chronicles?

Ans. A chronicle is a record of the rule of the kings and life at the court. Most kings had court chroniclers who wrote in detail about what happened during their reign.

Q5.2 What new technology were brought into the India during the medieval period and how did it bring about economic change in the society?

1. In irrigation, the Persian wheel came to be used.

2. The spinning wheel made weaving clothes easier.

3. In combat, firearms came to be used.

4. For writing, paper was introduced.

Q5.3 which kind of information can be obtained from archaeological sources of the medieval period?

Ans. The archaeological and literary sources of information help historians trace history. Archaeological sources include monuments, temples, inscriptions, coins and weapons. Literary sources include manuscripts, folk tales, poems and biographies of different rulers.

Q5.4 What is the tripartite struggle? Among which kingdom it take place?

Ans. The Tripartite Struggle also known as The Kannauj Triangle Wars for control of northern India took place in the ninth century, among the Pratihara Empire, the Pala Empire and the Rashtrakuta Empire.

Q6.1 Name any four important writing of the period and say which ruler reign writing describe?

Ans. 1. Abul Fazal's Akbarnama describe reign of Akbar.

2. Jahangir's Tuzuk-i-jahangiri describe reign of Jahangir.

3. Gulbadan begum's humayun nama which was written in the reign of humayun

4. Babur's Baburnama which was written in the reign of babur.

Q6.2 Name the kingdom that emerged in the north and those that were established in the south?

Ans. The kingdom that emerged in the north Rajput, Sikh, Maratha, Ahom, Jaat and In south the Cholas emerged powerful.

Q6.3 Why was India known as Bharat? How did it come to be known as Hindustan? How did Babur describe India?

Ans. The name Bharat as derived from the name of Bharat, son of the a legendary ruler mentioned in the Mahabharata. Babur used the term Hindustan to describe the subcontinent Hindustan became synonym with India only during British Raj.

CHAPTER TWO

EMERGENCE OF NEW KINGDOMS

Chapter-2 Emergence of new Kingdoms

Q1. Who wons the First battle of Tarain?

Ans. king Prithviraj Chauhan

Q2. Name two greatest rulers of the Cholas Empire?

Ans. Rajaraja Chola I and Rajendra Chola I were the greatest rulers of the Chola dynasty,

Q3. Which three empire participated in tripartite struggle?

Ans. The Tripartite Struggle also known as The Kannauj Triangle Wars for control of northern India took place in the ninth century, among the Pratihara Empire, the Pala Empire and the Rashtrakuta Empire.

Q4. What are brahmadeyas?

Ans. Brahmadeya (given to Brahmana) was tax free land gift either in form of single plot or whole villages donated to Brahmanas in the early medieval India. It was initially practiced by the ruling dynasties and was soon followed up by the chiefs, merchants, feudatories, etc

Q5. Which ruler built the Kailash Temple at Ellora?

Ans. Krishan- I

Q6. Write a note on chola village assemblies?

Ans. The Cholla Village assemblies- Ur , Sabha/Mashabha,Nagaram played an important role in village administration. deciding among its crucial matters

- The Ur-was an assembly of common villages.
- The sabha/Masabha was for the brahmeydas- brahmin villages
- The Nagarams were for the local merchants and traders gathering.

Q7. How many times did Mahmud Ghazni invaded from India? What was his main aim?

Ans. Mahmud Ghazni invaded India 17 times. Mahmud of Ghazni launched a number of raids on the Indian subcontinent. The primary aim of these raids was to acquire wealth, to finance the campaigns in central Asia and to strengthen the empire. His literal aim was to loot money.

Q8. Explian the tripartite struggle in your own words?

Ans. The Tripartite Struggle also known as The Kannauj Triangle Wars for control of northern India took place in the ninth century, among the Pratihara Empire, the Pala

Q9.. Explain the new kingdoms rose to power in the early medieval period. Give example of one such kingdom.

Ans. In the post Gupta period, administrative officials were also granted land. These officials owed fiscal and military obligations to the rulers. Land grants grew in numbers in the seventh century and become widespread throughtout the country. Such land officials also known as feudatories. However, the feudatory chiefs were eager to free themselves whenever there was an opportunity. Some of these feudatories struggled and rose to form new kingdoms during the early Medieval period. For example, the Palas were dominant in eastern India.

Q10. In your own words, describe the achievement of Rajaraja I and Rajendra I?

Ans. Under the king Rajaraja Chola I and Rajendra Chola I, the empire became powerful in the field of army, finance and culture in South Asia and South-east Asia. Raja Raja Chola (985-1014 AD) was the greatest ruler of this dynasty.

His empire consisted of whole of southern India, Sri Lanka, and parts of the Malay peninsula (modern Malaysia) and the Sumatran-based Srivijaya Kindgom (modern Indonesia).

After that Rajaraja Chola I and Rajendra Chola I the two great king of the dynasty, expanded the kingdom outside the traditional limits of a Tamil State, from the Sri Lankan island in the south to the Godavari-Krishna River basin in the north with the Konkan coast in Bhatkal, the total Malabar Coast including Lakshadweep, Maldives and huge range of Chera Empire.

The Cholas had a good architectural sense and it is found today in different place of south India. They built a number of Siva temples alongside the banks of the river Kaveri. The Airavateswara temple at Darasuram is a traditional example of Chola art and architecture. Rajaraja Chola and his son Rajendra Chola I had established two temples in Thanjavur and Gangaikondacholapuram. The superb Siva temple of Thanjavur was completed around 1009 AD; it was a great achievement of the time of Rajaraja. The largest and tallest of all Indian temples of its time was the temple of Gangaikondacholisvaram which was created by Rajendra Chola in around 1030 AD.

Q11. The chola dynasty was powerful because of its able administration. Describe the main features of administration of the chola kingdom with special mention of the village administration.

Ans. The most important feature of the Chola administration was the local administration at districts, towns and villages level. Uttaramerur inscriptions speak much about the Chola administration. Village autonomy was the most unique feature of Chola administrative system.

Q12. Fill in the blanks"-

1. The tripartite struggle was a battle between **the pala, Pratihara and Rashtrakutas** for the control over fertile region of Gangetic valley.

2. The **nagarams** was an assembly of merchants and belonged to the localitites where traders and merchants were in a dominant position.

3. One of the first and most prominent invaders in India in the medieval period was **Mahmud Ghazni.**

4. Temple architecture methods its peak under the kingdom of **Cholas.**

5. **Al Biruni** accompanised Mahmud of Ghazni to India during various raids.

6. Administrative officials who were granted land by the rulers were known as **feudatories.**

7. The pratihara dynasty flourished the most under the rule of **Mihir Bhoj** and his successor **Mahendra pala.**

8. In 1025 Mahmud Ghazni attacked, looted and demolished **the hindu temple of Somnath.**

9. **Rajaraja-I** defeated the Cheras and seized Madurai.

10. The **Chauhan** were the most prominent among the Rajput kniigdoms that emerged during the early medieval period.

DELHI SULTANATE

<u>**Chapter-3 Delhi Sultanate**</u>
<u>**FILL IN THE BLANKS:-**</u>

1. Razia Sultan had to step down from the throne because <u>**she was a women in a man's world.**</u>
2. Balban was the ruler of the <u>**Slave**</u> Dynasty.
3. Heavily fortified towns with the presence of soldiers were known as <u>**garrison town.**</u>
4. After the Tughlaq, the Sultanate was ruled by <u>**Sayyids.**</u>
5. Muhammad Bin Tughlaq introduced a token currency of bronze coin to be used in place of silver coin called <u>**tanka.**</u>
6. <u>**Balban**</u> was the last important ruler of slave dynasty.
7. Kharaj was the land tax imposed by <u>**Alauddin Khalji**</u> to increase revenue.
8. <u>**Shahna-i-mandi**</u> was the person who controlled the market.
9. Muhammad Bin Tughlaq shifted the capital of his empire from Delhi to <u>**Daulatabad.**</u>
10. <u>**Alauddin Khalji**</u> Reassessed land tax.

<u>**State TRUE/ FALSE**</u>

1. Qutub-ud-din Aibek established the slave dynasty. == T
2. Mongols began to appear on the borders of India during the reign of Razia Sultan. == F
3. The sultan of Delhi Sultnate was not dependent on Bandagans. == F
4. Razia Sultan was the only women ruler of the Delhi sultanate. == T
5. Muhhamad bin Tughlaq was the most learned man of the Delhi sultanate. == T

<u>Ques1. Name three prominent sultan's of slave dynasty?</u>

Ans. The three prominent sultan of slave dynasty are:-

1. Qutub-ud-din Aibak
2. Shams-ud-din Iltumish
3. Ghiyas-ud-din Balban

<u>Ques2. What were the chalgans?</u>

Ans. The chalgans were a board of forty nobles appointed by Iltumish of the Slave dynasty. They were very powerful and were well-known to sultan.

<u>Ques3. Name the five dynasty of the Delhi Sultanate?</u>

Ans. The five dynasty of Delhi sultanate are:-

1. Slave Dynasty (1206-1290)
2. Khalji Dynasty (1290-1320)
3. Tughlaq Dynasty (1320-1414)
4. Sayyid Dynasty (1414-1451)
5. Lodhi Dynasty (1451-1526)

<u>Ques 4. Who were Muqtis?</u>

Ans. The military commander who were appointed as governor of the territories of varying sizes or land holders of iqta were known as muqtis. Their duty was to lead military campaigns and maintain law and order in their iqtas.

<u>Ques 5. What are Garrison Town?</u>

Ans. Garrison Town is a common expression for any town that has military base nearby. A town fortified with the settlements of soldiers was known as Garrison Town.

<u>Ques 6. Why was the increase in land tax imposed by Muhammad Bin Tughlaq ill-timed?</u>

Ans. He increased the tax on the Doab are which was very fertile. It was the are located between the Ganga and the Yamuna river. The tax was increases at the time when monsoon failed and agriculture failed miserably. This led to famine and death of several farmers.

<u>Ques 7. What steps did Alauddin khalji take to discourage corruption?</u>

Ans. Steps taken by Alauddin Khalji to control corruption are;-

1. Muqtis were appointed to lead military campaign and maintain law and order in the iqtas. They collect revenue of their assignments as salary.
2. Muqtis were controlled by not allowing them inheritable position or assingning their iqtas for a short period of time.
3. Accountants were appointed by the state to check the amount of revenue collected by the muqtis.
4. Care was taken that the muqtis collected only the tax prescribed by the state and that he kept the required number of soldiers.
5. Alauddin khalji brought the assessment and collection of land revenue under his control.
6. The right of the local chieftains to levy taxes were cancelled and they were also forced to pay taxes.
7. There were three type of taxes:- kharaj (land cultivation), cattle and house.

Ques8. Why did Delhi sultanate disintegrate after the Tughlaqs?
Ans. Causes of the disintegrate of the Tughlaq Dynasty:-

1. Five failed plans of Muhammad Tughlaq
2. No definite law of succession
3. Autocratic ruler
4. No efforts to win hindu
5. Unwieldy empire
6. Poor financial position
7. Paucity of faithful and able commanders and advisers.
8. Selfishness of the Amirs.

Ques9. Why was Iltumish daughter removed from the throne?
Ans. Razia Sultan was removed from the throne in 1240CE. Because pople during the age were not comfortable having queen as a ruler. They regarded women to be inferior to men and hence not fit to rule over the people. Also the noble were not happy at her attempts to rule independently.

Ques 10. Why did Muhammad Bin Tughlaq drop the idea of developing as a second or alternative capital?
Ans. By the time people reach Daulatabad Muhammad bin Tughlaq changed his mind and decided to abandon the new capital and move to his old capital Delhi. Because he realized that it was difficult to control South

India from Delhi, it was equally difficult to control Delhi while sitting in Daulatabad. It ia believed that he wished to shift the capital as safeguard measure from Mongols.

Ques 11. Describe Alauddin Khalji rule with special mention to market reforms and administration?

Ans. Administration :- an Iqta and Muqti was appointed to collect the land revenue. He relied on the iqta system of administration.

He ensure that the officers were not hereditary. Officials were transferred frequently so that they had minimal social and political connection with the public. Initially Kharaj was kept at 1/6 of the produce he raised it to 50%. He also collects cattle and house tax. This is used for huge army.

Prices of all commodities were fixed. To keep track of the market price a special officer or Shahna-i-mandi was appointed. He took all the possible steps to increase the revenue of his kingdom.

Ques 12. Identify the reasons for the failure of Muhammad Bin Tughlaq projects?

Ans. The reason for failure are:-

1. The timing of implementation of his administrative policies was very wrong. Eg. He raised land tax in the Doab region 50% of the produce at the time when the area was under the grip of famine. People were unable to make payments. Which led to a revolt. He transferres his capital from Delhi to Daulatabad to contol South and North India. But later he realized that it was difficult to manage northern part of his kingdom.

2. Muhammad Bin Tughlaq introduced token currency called Tanka. But his experiment proved to beg failure. Over the time the silver currency was replaced by forged homemade coins. This resulted into monetary loss.

THE MUGHAL EMPIRE

Chapter-4 The Mughal Empire.
Fill in the blanks:-

1. Jahangir's wife name was **Mehrunnisa**
2. **Akbar** introduced the mansabdari system.
3. The **mansabdari** system introduces by Akbar was system that dealt with military administration.
4. The land revenue system that developed during the reign of Akbar was called **zabti.**
5. **Aurangzeb** is best known for his Deccan and foreign policy.
6. Humayun sought help of the Persian king Shah Tahmasp to conquer **Delhi and Agra.**
7. Akbar defeated Hemu the wazir of the Sur dynasty in the second battle of **Panipat.**
8. Aurangzeb captured the last of Sia states Bijapur ans **Golconda.**
9. **William Hawkings** visited the court of Jahangir in 1615.
10. Jalaludin Akbar was only thirteen year old at the time of **Humayun's** death.

Match the column

Mansabdar == Officer of the Mughal army
Diwan-i-kul == Responsible for revenue and finance
Qazi-ul-qazzat == Head of judiciary
Mir Bakhi == Looked after the military
Sadr-us sadar == Protected the laws of shar'at
State T/F

1. Taj Mahal was built by Humayun. ==**F**

2. Rana Sanga, the king of Mewar defeated Babur. == **F**
3. Aurangzeb assumed the title of Alamgir. == **T**
4. Nadir Shah invasion in 1739 weakened the Mughal empire. ==**T**
5. The Mir Bakshi was in charge of the military. == **F**

Q1. Name the six main rulers of the Mughal Dynasty?

Ans. The six rulers of Mughal Dynasty are- Babur, Humayun, Akbar, Jahangir, Shahjahan, and Aurangzeb

Q2. Akbarnama and Ain-i-Akbari autobiographies of which ruler?

Ans. Akbar

Q3. Who encouraged Babur to attack India?

Ans. Daulat Khan Lodi

Q4. Which Mughal ruler brought almost the whole of India under his control?

Ans. Akbar

Q5. Where was the first English trading post established in India?

Ans. Surat

Q 6. Which Mughal ruler developed the idea of Sulh-i-kul or 'universal peace'?

Ans. Akbar

Q7. Trace the origin of Mughals?

Ans. The word Mughal was derived from the word "Mongols". The Mughal claimed to be the descendants of Genghis Khan, the ruler of Mongol Tribe, they were the fifth generation descendant of Timur, the ruler of Iran, Iraq and Turkey.

Q8. Explain the statement: The Mughals followed the Timurid tradition of succession?

Ans. The succession treatment of Mughals was not that of primogeniture. Instead they followed the Mughal and Timurid custom of coparcenary inherit, the inheritance is divided among all sons.

Q9. Who was Akbar's regent? What role did he play in the politics of the time?

Ans. Biram Khan was Akbar's regent. He was the commander in chief of Mughal's Army, Guardian and mentor of Akbar. The role played by him are:-

1. He served Humayun and his Son Akbar and made efforts to expand Mughal empire.

2. After the death of Humayun he became the regent of the throne, as Akbar was too young.
3. He consolidates Mughal Authority in Northern India.
4. He led the Mughal forces at the Second battle of Panipat to defeat Hemu, the wazir of Sur Dynasty.

Q10. Mughal and Rajputs entered into matrimonial alliances. How did Mughals use this to bring about stability in their kingdoms?

Ans. Rajput's were the most powerful rivals of Mughal in Northern India. Knowing this Akbar adopted a special policy to handle the Rajputs. He was a far sighted ruler who knew that there could be no permanent ruler of Mughal Empire without the support of Rajput's. Akbar wanted to be friendly with Rajput instead of subjugating. For this he adopted all possible measures like matrimonial alliances and assigning higher posts to Rajput chiefs. This made his position stronger and became his loyal comrades.

Q11. How did the frequent transfer of officials ensure effective administration?

Ans. In Mughal empire the Jagirs collected the revenue from the Zamindars on the behalf of Mansabdars. The Jagirs were transferred frequently to instil a sense of insecurity in them and prevent them from becoming powerful. Apart from the frequent transfer, even the hereditary claim to the personal property was disallowed in proportion to the revenue the late mansabdar owned to the state.

Q12. Write a note on Mughal administration?

Ans. The military Administration or the mansabdari system was the backbone of the Mughal Empire which started in its crude from the Zahir-us-din Babur its refine form in the reign of Akbar. Each mansabdar kept his own army according to his rank and manage the recruitment, training and salaries of the soldiers. The Mughal followed the custom of the co-parcenary inheritance, where parental property is equally divided among his all sons. As the mughal became powerful several rulers voluntarily submitted to their authority. Many Rajput rulers married their daughter to the Mughal families to gain position in Mughal Court.

Q13. Explain Akbar's religious policy?

Ans. Akbar's Liberal religious view and his marriage to the Rajput princess influence his religious outlook. He used to hold task with the leader of various religions. He also built a building called Ibadat khana at Agra to hold religious talk with leaders. Views were exchanged freely. He also introduced the policy of sulh-i-kul. This idea of tolerance focused on honesty, justice and peace that were universaly applicable. Akbar taught all religion have similar ideology. Thus he incorporates the principles of all to found a new faith which he named Din-ai-Ilahi. Din-Ai-Ilahi did not attract many converts and it perished with the death of Akbar.

Q14. How was Aurangzeb's rule different from that of his predecessors?

Ans, Unlike predecessor Unlike his predecessors, Aurangzeb wanted that the sharia or Islamic law to be followed everywhere and the practices against the Islam rules, such as the consumption of alcohol and gambling, to be disallowed in the public. Unlike his predecessors, his reign was marked by austerity. The monumental architecture that characterised the reigns of Akbar and Shah Jahan, including the Agra Fort, Fatehpur Sikri, the Taj Mahal and Shahjahanabad, held little interest for Aurangzeb, and similarly the musicians who had adorned the courts of his predecessors were dismissed.

Q15. What were the major factors that led to the decline of the Mughal Empire?

Ans. 1- Rise of independent states. 2- Wars of succession 3- Foreign invaders 4- Negative roles of nobles

CHAPTER FIVE

SOCIAL CHANGES IN MEDIEVAL PERIOD

CHAPTER- 5 SOCIAL CHANGES IN MEDIEVAL PERIOD

<u>Multiple choices the question:-</u>

1. Rani durgavati belonged to the **<u>Gond tribe</u>** .
2. People belonging to the khokar tribe lived in **<u>Punjab</u>**.
3. **<u>Oral traditions</u>** are the main source of information that historians use to study tribal history.
4. The first major expansion of the Ahom tribe, which was annexed in 1522, was under the leadership of **<u>suhungmung</u>** .
5. Banjaras were the most important **<u>trader-nomads</u>** during the medieval period.

<u>Fill in the blanks:-</u>

1. Rajputs emerged from **tribal** groups.
2. Rathyatra festival is celebrated every year in puri to worship **<u>lord jagnath</u>**.
3. The sultan was at the top of the political set up and below him were the **<u>ulima amirs</u>**.
4. Many tribes, obtained their livelihood from **<u>agriculture.</u>**
5. Ahom society was divided into **<u>clams.</u>**

<u>True /False</u>

1. The tribes did not usually preserve their culture. **F**

2. Kamal khan Gakkhar was made a mansabdar by the Mughal emperor Jahangir. **F**
3. The original homeland of the Ahoms was Burma. **F**
4. Banjaras were settled agriculturists. **F**
5. The kolis and numerous other tribes inhabited the Maharashtra highlands. **T**

Q1.Why do we know so little about the tribal societies and groups of the medieval period?

Ans:- The language of most tribal communities have not developed a script of their own and thus no information is recorded.

Q2. Differentiate between nomads and itinerant groups?

Ans:- Nomads are wandering pastoralists who roam from one pasture to another with their families and herd of cattle. Craftsmen, traditional from place to place practice their different occupations.

Q3. Where did Ahoms established their kingdom?

Ans:- The Ahoms established the Ahom kingdom in parts of present-day Assam and ruled it for nearly 600 years.

Q4. Who was Genghis khan?

Ans:- Genghis khan, the ruler of Mongol tribes of china and central Asia.

Q5. Which tribes were significant in Punjab?

Ans. Tribes that were significant in Punjab were Khokhar, and Gokkhars.

Q6. Who were the Gonds?

Ans. The Gonds were one of the most important tribal groups in central India during the medieval period. The area under their control was between Jabalpur and Bhopal.

Q7. Mention the names of a few tribes that emerged during the medieval period. Write where were they established?

Ans. Few tribes that emerged during the medieval period:-

1. The Bhils were one the most widely spread communities across western and central India.
2. The Gonds were located across the present day states of Chhattisgarh, Madhya Pradesh, Maharashtra and Andhra Pradesh.
3. The Mundad and Santhals were the other important tribes that lived in Odisha, Jharkhand and Bengal.

Q8. Who was Rani Durgawati?

Ans. Rani Durgawati ruled the origin during the sixteenth century on behalf of her five year old son. After the death of her husband. She refused to go before Akbar and fought, the huge Mughal forces she was wounded in battle and preferred to stab herself to death rather than be captured and dishonored by the Mughal army.

Q9. Write about the style of warfare of the Ahoms?

Ans. Ahoms domination spread the limits of the Mughal power in the north east region. They were able to mobilize all adults males for military service, what is known as the militia system. The Ahoms state taxes and organized people by labor levies and produce rather than land revenue. The Mughals found this style of origination extremely difficult to combat.

Q10. State three differences between the culture of the tribes and that of the Hindus?

Ans. Three differences between the culture of the tribes and that of the Hindus are:-

1. Tribal people lived in forest area. Hindus groups lived in plain areas.
2. Tribal society believed in only two forces of nature and Hindus society worship specific god and goddess.
3. Tribal people followed their tradition and their own language. Hindus followed their own tradition but different language.

Q11. How did the Ahom state organize its people and administration?

Ans. Ahom society was divided into clans or Khels which generally held so way over several villages. The peasant were given land by the village community. This land could not be taken away by the king without the consent of the community. Poets and scholars were given land grants and their work was appreciated. Artisans were scare in the Ahoms area and they mostly come from neighboring kingdoms. In the Ahoms kingdom encouragement was given to theatre.

Q12. Write a note on tribal livelihood?

Ans. Many tribes obtained their livelihood from agriculture. Others were hunters, gathres or harder's. Most often they combined these activities to make full use of the natural resources of the area where they lived some tribes were nomads and moved from one place to another. Similarly the nomadic pastoralist moved from one place to another with their animals. They exchange wool, ghee, milk, etc. with settled agriculture for grains, cloths and other needs. They bought and sold these goods as they moved from one place to another transporting them on their animals.

RELIGIOUS IDEA IN MEDIEVAL PERIOD

Chapter =6 (Religious Idea in Medieval Period).
Fill in the blanks:-

1. Sufism introduced many popular orders **of silsilahs.**
2. **Chaitanya** disregard for caste distinction in the sphere of devotional singing promoted a sense of equality in Bengal Life.
3. The Guru Granth Sahib is the holy scripture of **Sikhs.**
4. Namdev's teching became so popular that they were later absorbed in the **Adi Grantha.**
5. Kabir belonged to a family of **weaver.**
6. The **Sufism** is a mystic tradition of Islam.
7. Mira Bai was a devotee of lord **Krishna.**
8. **Ramananda** was the most prominent scholar saint of the Vaishnava bhakti in northern India during the Sultanate period.
9. The teaching of **Guru Nanak Dev.** led to the emergence of Sikhism.
10. A separate group called **Kabirpanthi** was formed by the follower of Kabirs.

State T/F?

1. The sufi path is called the Tariqa. == **T**
2. The Adi Grantha is a religious book of the Sufis. == **F**
3. Sikhism was founded by Guru Arjan Dev. == **F**
4. The word " Sufi" comes from the word suf. == **F**
5. The Maharashtra bhakti tradition drew its basic inspiration from Bhagawat Gita Purana. == **T**

Q1. What is Bhakti?

Ans. Bhakti is the devotion toward a God or his various forms.

Q2. Who formed the kabirpanthis?

Ans. Kabirpanthis formed by the followers of Kabir includes Hindus and Muslims.

Q3. What is the Shariat?

Ans. Muslim Holy Law was called Shariat.

Q4. Name a few monotheistic saints?

Ans. Guru Nanak Dev, Namdev, Kabir, Mirabai .

Q5. What were the three principles that according to Guru Nanak formed the essence of life?

Ans. Three principles according to Guru Nanak were:-

1. Worship of one God.
2. He insisted that caste, creed or gender were irrelevant for attaining liberation.
3. His idea of liberation was not that state of inert bliss but rather the pursuit of active life with a strong sense of social commitment.

Q6. Write short notes on the two styles of Indian Classical Music?

Ans. The two important genres of Indian classical music are Carnatic music and Hindustani music. Carnatic music is one of the oldest forms of classical music and is related to the Southern part of India

Q7. Write a note on Guru Nanak's teaching?

Ans. The most famous teachings attributed to Guru Nanak are that there is only one God, and that all human beings can have direct access to God with no need of rituals or priests. His most radical social teachings denounced the caste system and taught that everyone is equal, regardless of caste or gender.

Q8. What did the monotheistic movement represent and in what manner was it different from Vaishnava Bhakti?

Ans. The monotheistic movement represented bhakti of only one God, ie; was non-incarnate and formless, eternal and ineffable. ... It was different from Vaishnava bhakti as monotheistic movement believed in one God which is formless, eternal whereas the Vaishnava bhakti believed in many Gods.

RISE OF AUTONOMOUS STATES IN THE 18TH CENTURY

Chapter-7 (Rise of autonomous states in the eighteenth century)
<u>**Fill in the blanks:-**</u>

1. The Jat kingdoms attained its zenith under <u>**Surajmal.**</u>
2. <u>**Maratha**</u> were defeated in the third battle of Panipat.
3. <u>**Nadir Shah,**</u> the ruler of Iran, plundered the city of Delhi in 1739 and carried away with him immense wealth.
4. It was <u>**Guru Gobind Singh**</u> who transformed the Sikhs into a warrior community.
5. The state of Hyderabad wa founded by <u>**Nizam Mulk Asaf Jah.**</u>
6. After Shivaji's death, the effective control of the Maratha kingdom fell into the hands of the <u>**Peshwas.**</u>
7. The <u>**Sardesh Mukhi**</u> was an additional levy of 10% demanded from areas outside the Maratha Kingdom.
8. <u>**Mazumdar**</u> looked into the income and expenditure of the Maratha state.
9. Jat kingdom reached its zenith under <u>**Gokula**</u> in 1669.
10. Regional power arose in Hyderabad under <u>**Nizam Mulk Asaf Sah**</u> after the decline of the Mughal power.

<u>**State T/ F?**</u>

1. Nadir Shah invaded India five times between 1748 and 1761<u>. == F</u>
2. The Jat kingdom attained its zenith under Surajmal. ==<u> T</u>

3. Shivaji emphasized on agriculture improvement thus benefitting all peasants. ==_T
4. The Maratha seized Malwa and Guajrat from the Mughals. ==F
5. Murshid Quli Khan transferred the capital of Awadh from Dhaka to Murshidabad. == _T

Q1. What do you understand by the jagidari crisis?

Ans The Jagirdari Crisis was an economic situation where there was a shortage of lands or jagirs. This defrayed the cost of administration and the imperial throne was unable to pay for wars or maintain a standard of living of its nobility. This resulted in the Mughal throne giving its own land to pay its officials.

Q2. Why were Jats employed as mercenary soldier by Hindu and Muslim Sikh?

Ans, the Jats were known for being hardy agriculturist brave warrior, and daring robbers of caravans. That is why they were employes as mercenary soldiers by the Hindu and Sikhs.

Q3. Define chauth and sadeshmukhi.

Ans. The chauth amounted to one-fourth of the standard revenue assessment of the place. The sardeshmikhi was an additional levy of the 10 percent demanded from areas outside his kingdom.

Q4. What were the reforms introduced by the Nizam of Hyderabad?

Ans. The reforms initiated by the Nizam included the establishment of peace and security by suppressing all disaffected nobles and putting down theft and robbery, efoorts to stop the plundering raids of the Marathas and rivals of agriculture and industry by giving incentives to farmers and craftsmen.

Q5. How did the formation of Khalsa help in the growth of Sikhs as a major regional power?

Ans.Guru Gobind Singh, the tenth and the last Sikhs guru transformed the Sikhs into a warrior community. Gobind Singh established the khalsa , or the brotherhood of the sikhs. The khalsa gives the community a deep sense of unity founded on symbolic acts.

Q6. Write a short note on Jats?

Ans. The Jats lived in areas of Haryana, Punjab, the western region of the Ganga-Yamuna Doab, and eastern Rajputana. The Jats attained political importance only in the later seventeenth century and early eighteenth century.

Q7. Nadir Shah invaded India several times. What was the extent of wealth plundered by him?

Ans. Nadir Shah plundered the city of Delhi in 1739 and carried away with him Immence wealth including Kohinoor diamond and the jewel studded peacock throne of Shahjahan.

Q8. Explain briefly the Maratha administration?

Ans. The Maratha polity was essentialy a centralized autocratic monarchy. To assist the king, there was a council of state minister known as ashtapradhan. Shivaji divided the territory directly under his rule into three provinces, each under a veciroy. He further divided the provinces into prants, each of which was subdivided inot parganas and tarafs. The lowest unit wa village and each village had its headmen or patel.

Q9. What are the common features of the three regional states of Bengal, Awadh and Hyderabad?

Ans. These three states were the major provinces during the british rule

.

Bengal ,awadh and hyderabad all three were major source of revenues and gave most of the contribution to revenue.

Apart from that all these three provinces were independent and powerful and but maintained their diplomatic relationship with the mughal emperor. These three regions framed the most of the part of Indian political system and most policies were mainly focussed to these three provinces.

OUR ENVIRONMENT

<u>Chapter-8 Our Environment</u>

<u>Ques. A. Fill In the Blanks:-</u>

1. The physical environment comprises of **<u>non-living</u>**components.
2. The environment is **<u>dynamic</u>**in nature.
3. 29% of the lithosphere is occupied by**<u>land.</u>**
4. **<u>Ozone</u>** protects us from the harmful ultraviolet rays of the Sun.
5. The great variety of life is on Earth is called **<u>biodiversity.</u>**
6. All energy of life comes from the**<u> Sun.</u>**

<u>Ques. B.1: What do you mean by environment?</u>

ANS.: Environment is the sum total of the surroundings and conditions within which a living organism exists. Land, water, air, plants and other living organisms constitute the environment.The components of environment can be divided into two groups: natural and human.The biological and physical environments of an organism form the natural environment. Human beings and their creations, such as bridges, roads and farms and the political, social and economic order in which they live, form the human environment.

<u>Ques. B.2: How is the lithosphere useful to us?</u>

ANS.: Lithosphere, also known as the crust, is the outermost solid layer of the Earth. It is a reservoir of resources that helps us in following ways:
i) It provides minerals and rocks that are used in construction and other industries.
ii) It is a source of fuels such as petroleum and natural gas.
iii) The lithosphere provides land for agriculture. This acts as a source of income as well as supply of food for human beings.
iv) The hydrosphere and the land provide nutrients to plants and animals. It

helps in their growth.

Ques. B.3: What is the hydrosphere comprised of?

ANS.: Hydrosphere is the total mass of water found on the surface of the Earth. Its components include ice sheets found in the mountainous regions and all the water bodies such as lakes, ponds, rivers, seas, oceans, underground water and the water vapour present in atmosphere.

Ques. B.4: What holds the atmosphere around the earth?

ANS.: Earth's gravitational pull holds the atmosphere around the Earth and prevents it from escaping into outer space. The force of the Earth's surface, which pulls things towards itself, is known as gravitational force. This force is strong enough to hold the molecules of gases present in atmosphere close to the Earth.

Ques. B.5: What is the significance of the biosphere?

ANS.: The sum total of land, water and air present on Earth is the called biosphere. It is the sum of all ecosystems in which living organisms are present.

The biosphere is important due to the following reasons:

i) Biosphere provides all living beings the necessary conditions for life such as suitable climate, water and air.

ii) Air is necessary for humans and animals to breathe and for plants to produce energy through photosynthesis.

iii) Water is also essential for sustaining life.

iv) Land provides with minerals and fuels and also helps in the survival of plants and trees.

Ques. B.6: What is an ecosystem?

ANS.: A distinct zone in the biosphere within which a community of living as well as non-living components exist and survive by mutual interaction is an called an ecosystem. The biotic or living components are human beings, plants, animals, trees and the abiotic components are land, water and air. Energy from the Sun is recycled by transferring matter as well as energy among the components. The process of change and transfer of energy makes anecosystem dynamic.

Ques. B.7: Why have human beings modified the environment?

ANS.: Human beings have adjusted their surroundings according to their needs. However, with the increase in population at an alarming rate, the demand of basic requirements such as food, houses and roads has also increased. Therefore, human beings have started altering the environment for the fulfilment of their requirements. Farming, grazing, construction of bridges, houses and roads and building industries and transport systems have helped human beings survive and lead a life of convenience.

Ques. C.1: Difference between Physical and biological environment.?

Physical Environment

1. Physical environment consists of non-living or abiotic components.

2. Land, air and water form the physical environment.

3. The Sun is the primary source of energy in the physical environment.

Biological Environment

1. Biological environment consists of living or biotic components.

2. Human beings, animals, plants, trees and other living creatures form the biological environment.

3. The Sun as well as the physical environment are the sources of energy in the biological environment.

Ques. C.2: Difference between Hydrosphere and atmosphere.

Hydrosphere

1. Hydrosphere is the total mass of water found on the Earth's surface.

2. Hydrosphere consists of lakes, oceans, rivers, seas, water vapours, underground water and ice sheets of the mountainous regions.

3. Hydrosphere influences climate through water cycle and precipitation.

Atmosphere

1. Atmosphere is the layer of air that envelopes the Earth.

2. Atmosphere consists of various gases such as nitrogen, oxygen, helium and ozone. Water vapours and dust particles are also a part of this layer.

3. Atmosphere influences climate by absorption of heat and movement of air.

Ques. C.3: Difference between Biosphere and ecosystem.

Biosphere

1. Biosphere is the sum total of the land, air and water on the Earth.

2. Biosphere consists of many ecosystems.

3. Biosphere has distinct components like hydrosphere, atmosphere and lithosphere.

Ecosystem

1. Ecosystem is a community or a distinct zone consisting of biotic and abiotic components.

2. Ecosystem is a distinct zone within the biosphere.

3. Ecosystem includes the interaction of all components of biosphere in a geographical region.

Ques. D.1: Explain with suitable examples, the interaction between physical and biological environment.

ANS.: The physical environment consists of all the abiotic elements of nature, that is, all the non living elements of nature, such as land, water and air. Physical environment derives most of its energy from the Sun. The biological environment, on the other hand, consists of all the living beings, such as humans, animals and micro-organisms. Elements of biological environment derive their energy from the physical environment. The biological and physical environments create a natural environment where they are interdependent.

1. Changes in physical environment affecting the biological environment: The physical environment can generate changes in the biological environment. For example, in case of a natural disaster in the physical environment, like landslide, the whole biotic environment of that place is affected. The ecosystem suffers in terms of its supply of food and relocation of inhabitants of an area. Another example emphasising changes in physical environment affecting the biological environment is the change in seasons and weather conditions . Due to the changes in the physical environment like increase or decrease in temperature or heavy or less rainfall, the biological elements of the ecosystem have to adapt themselves accordingly. For example, some animals go into hibernation during winters and humans change their clothing according to the change in climate.

2. Biological environment affecting the physical environment: The biotic environment can also generate changes in the physical environment. For example, hills are cut into steps for step farming, irrigation is done and the soil is loosened. Such changes are brought by the biological environment to the physical environment. Beavers build artificial dams out of wood to create a homes for themselves by blocking the rivers and changing the physical environment around them.

Hence, it can be seen that both the physical and the biological environments are in a constant state of interaction with each other.

Ques. D.2: What is ecological balance and why do we need to maintain it?

ANS.: The organisms in an ecosystem have their own physical environment. The living components interact with each other, transferring matter and energy among themselves as well as to the abiotic elements. The Sun is the source of energy for all life forms. Therefore, the ecosystem goes through constant change and the energy is recycled. Maintenance of an equilibrium in the transfer of energy and matter is known asecological balance. This balance helps to keep the ecosystem stable.

When there is more emission of energy and matter out of the ecosystem, an imbalance is created. This causes disruption in the proper functioning of the ecosystem. With the passage of time, the needs of human beings are increasing. This is leading to deforestation, loss of habitat of animals, increase in construction and transportation and industrialisation, which, in turn, is resulting into depletion of the ecosystem.

The ecological balance can be maintained in the following ways:

i) Controlling air and water pollution
ii) Preventing deforestation
iii) Stopping the hunting and poaching of animals to conserve the endangered species.
iv) Management of natural resources: Minerals, fossil fuels and other natural resources are being depleted very fast. These should be used carefully. This would ensure a better future with stable supply of natural resources.
v) Reuse and recycle: Water and other resources can be reused and recycled to prevent over consumption.

<u>Ques. D.3: Describe the composition of the atmosphere and mention the uses of its constituent gases.</u>

ANS.: Atmosphere is the layer of air that surrounds the Earth. The molecules of the gases are held close to the surface by the gravitational pull of the Earth. The atmosphere comprises the following components:

1. Gases
i) Nitrogen,which is the most abundant gas in the atmosphere and constitutes 78% of the air.
ii) Oxygen constitutes 21% of the air.
iii) Ozone, Hydrogen, Argon and Helium constitute 1% of the air.

2. Water vapour

3. Dust particles

The uses of the above mentioned constituent gases are as follows:

i) Nitrogen: It is used to make fertilisers and dyes. It is also used as a refrigerant as well as to store food.

ii) Oxygen: All living organisms use oxygen for breathing and hence, it is important for the survival of all life forms on Earth.

iii) Carbon dioxide: It is used by plants for producing energy through photosynthesis.

iii) Hydrogen helps in the formation of water.

iv) Ozone protects the Earth from the harmful ultraviolet rays of the Sun.

v) Argon is used for arc welding.

vi) Helium is used as a light weight aircraft fuel.

Ques. D.4: Why do we need to protect our environment?

ANS.: Environment includes the conditions and surroundings in which all life forms, humans, animals and plants live in. Land, water, air and all the components around us are a part of the environment. These help us to survive and nourish ourselves and help in our growth as well. We need to protect our environment because of the following reasons:

i) Increasing needs and demands are disrupting the balance in the environment.

ii) Increasing deforestation is causing loss of habitat as well loss of supply of food.

iii) Excessive construction is leading to the excessive use of natural resources like minerals and fuels.

iv) Increasing vehicles are depleting the resources of oil at an alarming rate.

v) Excessive farming and grazing is causing harm to the productivity of land, which, in turn causes, is creating a scarcity of resources to sustain life.

vi) The necessity to maintain and protect our environment emerges from the need for a healthy survival. Maintaining a clean and healthy environment not only increases aesthetic beauty of the surroundings but also contributes in maintaining good health.

Ques. D.5: Enlist some of the environment problems of your neighbourhood and write their solutions.

ANS.: Some of the environmental issues that the people are facing nowadays are created by themselves. People are disregarding the environmental needs for their own convenience. This has led to a polluted environment. Some of the key problems that my neighbourhood faces due to the ignorance of people are listed below along with their suitable solutions:

1. Excessive garbage on the streets: Some people do not put any effort in keeping the roads and the streets clean. They throw away garbage wherever they find it convenient. They litter the streets and do not use the dustbins that are provided for garbage disposal.

Solution: The solution to this problem is very simple; people only need to make the effort to throw the garbage in the nearest dustbin and not on the street. If a dustbin is not available nearby, then they can keep the waste that is to be disposed with them and throw it in the garbage bin at home.

2. Urinating in public: Some people do not have basic decency and pollute the environment by urinating wherever they please. This leads to spreading of diseases and a general unhygienic atmosphere.

Solution: People should have a sense of not polluting public places by urinating in public and should avoid such acts as they are unhygienic and harmful for the environment.

3. Improper drainage system: Some of the localities nearby have open drains that sometimes overflow on the streets. This leads to dirty water overflowing on the streets and transmission of diseases.

Solution: The drains should be covered, as it is not hygienic to come in contact with germs that breed in the drains and cause diseases and pollute the air around us.

THE STRUCTURE OF EARTH

Chapter-9 The structure of Earth

Q1. Fill in the blanks:-

1. The **crust** is the outermost layer of the earth.
2. Rocks containing metals in large quantities are called **ores.**
3. **Diamond** is the hardest mineral.
4. **Obsidian** is a good example of extrusive rock.
5. The temperature in the lower mantle is **2200 C.**
6. The core of earth is made up of **iron and nickel.**
7. Haematite is an ore **of iron**.
8. Sedimentary rocks are also called **stratified** rocks.
9. **Quartzite** is formed from Sedimentary rocks.

Q2. Match the following

Sima == Oceanic crust

Sial == Continental crust

Nife == Inner core

Magma ==Molten rocks

Q3. Name the three layers of earth?

Ans. Crust, Mantle, Core

Q4. What are minerals?

Ans. *Minerals* are substances naturally formed in the Earth. *Minerals* are typically solid, inorganic, have a crystal structure and are formed by geological process

Q5. How is lava different from magma?

Magma

1. The molten rock that is present beneath the surface of the earth is termed as Magma.

2. The temperature of Magma is slightly hotter and ranges from 1300-2400 degrees Fahrenheit.

3. The word Magma has its origins from Ancient Greek.

4. Magma takes much longer time in cooling, as it is located underground which leads to the creation of gigantic crystals

Lava

1. The molten liquid that gets erupted out of the surface of the Earth is termed as Lava. Lava is also referred to as Liquid Magma.

2. The temperature of Lava is slightly colder and ranges between 1300-2200 degrees Fahrenheit.

3. The word Lava has its origins from the Italian Language.

4. Lava has the property of cooling much quicker than magma. This leads to lava sometimes crystallizing into a glass

Q5. Why igneous rocks are called primary rocks?

Ans. *Igneous rocks are known* as *primary rocks* because they were the first ones to be formed in the rock cycle and do not contain any organic remains.

Q6. Which rock are also called stratified rock and why?

Ans. Sedimentary rocks are formed by deposition of sediments. After millions of years when these sediments are under an "extremely high pressure and temperature" they solidify to form **sedimentary rocks**. When these rock pieces are cut, the layers or strata are visible and hence it is called **stratified rocks.**

Q7. Define fossils?

Ans. *Fossils* are the remains or traces of ancient life that have been preserved by natural processes. Eg. Shell, bone, coal etc.

Q8. Difference between Intrusive and Extrusive rocks?

Intrusive Igneous Rocks

1. Intrusive igneous rocks are formed when the magma cools and solidify below the surface of the Earth.

2. Since these rocks cools down slowly, they have coarse texture with large crystals

3. **Example:** Dolomite

Extrusive Igneous Rocks

1. Extrusive igneous rocks are formed by cooling the molten magma on the surface of the Earth. The molten magma comes on to the Earth's surface through cracks, fissures and volcanic eruption

2. Since these rocks solidify at a faster pace, they are smooth, crystalline and fine grained.

3. **Example:** Basalt

Q9. How are sedimentary rocks found?

Ans. Sedimentation is the combined name for all the processes that cause organic and mineral particles to get settle. The particle that helps in forming the sedimentary rock is called **sediment**. This sediment is formed with the help of erosion and weathering from the source area and which is then transported to the deposition place by the wind, water, ice and glaciers which are agents of denudation.

Q10. Describe the structure of earth?

Ans. Earth is composed of many layers.

1)**Crust**- it is the outermost layer of earth. it is rich in silica.

2)**Mantle**- the layer below crust also called athenosphere. it is composed of molten rocks .

3)**Core**-it is the innermost layer of earth. it is composed of mainly nickel and iron.

Q11. Why do igneous and sedimentary rocks sometimes get changed? What are the new rocks called?

Ans. *sedimentary rock is subjected to heat (greater than 150 degree Celcius) and pressure (greater than 1500 bars), it changes into new a new type of rock. The new rock type is called metamorphic rock. Examples are change of granite into gneiss and the change of shale into slate.*

Q12. List the different uses of rocks?

Ans, 1.Making Cement == (Limestone) (Sedimentary Origin)

2.Fire == (Coal) (Sedimentary Origin)

3.Writing === (Chalk) (Sedimentary Origin)

4.Building Material == (Sandstone) (Sedimentary Origin)

5.Bath Scrub == (Pumice) (Igneous Origin)

6.Kerb Stone == (Granite) (Igneous Origin)

7.Roofing Material == (Slate) (Metamorphic Origin)

8.Statue/Ornaments/Decoration == (Marble) (Metamorphic Origin)

9.Valuable source of minerals (Gold, Diamond, Sapphire e.t.c)

10.Some rocks acts as tourist attraction sites.

COMPOSITION & STRUCTURE OF ATMOSPHERE

Chapter =10 (composition and structure of atmosphere)

A. Choose the correct answer and fill in the blanks.

1 .The lowest layer of the atmosphere is...**Troposphere**

2 .The uppermost layer of the atmosphere is.. **Exosphere**

3. The approximate height of the atmosphere is.. **1600 km**

4. All weather phenomena take place in the.. **Troposphere**

B. State whether true or false .If false ,correct the statement.

1. The atmosphere is held around the earth due to Earths gravitational pull. = **True**

2. Hydrogen gas makes up about 21% of the air. = **False**

3. In the stratosphere ,temperature decreases with increasing height. = **False**

4. Electrically charged particles are called ions. = **True**

C. Fill in the blanks.

1. The blanket of air surrounding the earth is called **Atmosphere**

2. Nitrogen is the main gas present in air, constituting about **78%** of it.

3. The troposphere extends to a height of about **18km** at the Equator.

4.The exosphere gradually merges with the**Interplanetary**space.

1. Name the five layers of the atmosphere.

Ans. The atmosphere is divided into five layers Troposphere , Stratosphere , Mesosphere ,Thermosphere and Exosphere.

2. What do you understand by the normal lapse rate?

Ans. The decrease in air temperature at the rate of 1'c for every 165 m increase in height.

3. How is the tropopause different from the stratopause?

Ans. The tropopause is a narrow boundary that seperates from the troposphere.

4. What is the significance of the ozone layer?

Ans. Ozone protects us from the harmful ultraviolet rays of the sun.

5. Which layer of the atmosphere makes radio communication possible?

Ans. Thermosphere

6. How is the troposphere important for us?

Ans. All weather phenomena, such as clouds ,fog , rainfall, snowfall ,storms and lightning , occur here. It absorbs maximum heat radiated by the Earth's surface and thus keeps the Earth warm.

7. Why is the thermosphere also called 'ionosphere'?

Ans. The thermosphere is also called ionosphere because of the presence of ions.

8. Difference between the mesosphere and thermosphere?

THERMOSPHERE

1. Thermosphere is the layer of the earth's atmosphere directly above the mesosphere and directly below the exosphere.
2. Temperature increases with increase in height.
3. The layer separating thermosphere and mesosphere is called mesopause.

MESOSPHERE

1. Mesosphere is layer of the earth's atmosphere that is directly above the stratosphere and directly below the thermosphere.
2. Temperature decreases with increase in height.
3. The layer separating mesosphere and stratosphere is called stratopause

Ques9 . Examine the significance of atmosphere?

Ans. The blanket of air surrounding the Earth is called the atmosphere. The significance of atmosphere is:-

1. Nitrogen is required for the fertility of soil.
2. Oxygen is required for all living beings to stay alive.

3. Carbon dioxide helps plants in food making process photosynthesis.
4. Ozone protects form harmful ultraviolet rays of sun.
5. Water vapor causes precipitation.

CHAPTER ELEVEN

NATURAL VEGETATION & WILDLIFE

Chapter- 11 Natural Vegetation and Wildlife.
Fill in the blanks :-

1. Rainforest are also known as **Selva**
2. Tropical deciduous forest not found in **Spain.**
3. **Rosewood** tree is not found in the coniferous forest.
4. Marsupials are found in **Australia.**
5. Seals and walruses are found in the sea adjoining the coast of the **Tundra.**
6. A natural vegetation zone which has wildlife unique to it is called a **biome.**
7. Tropical evergreen forests are found in the **Equatorial region**.
8. The **giant panda** of china is well known animal of the temperate evergreen.
9. Coniferous forest are also known as **Taiga**
10. Xerophytic plants are found in the **hot desert.**

State T/F?

1. Natural vegetation includes the plants tht grow naturally in a particular area. == **T**
2. Teak and Sal tree are commercially very valuable. == **T**
3. Eucalyptus and mulberry trees are found in Sweden. == **F**
4. Fur-bearing animal are found in the coniferous forest. == **T**
5. The grassland of the Brazilian Highlands are called Savannah. == **F**

Q1. What are the factors that determine the type of vegetation found in a region?

Ans. The factors that determine the type of vegetable found in a region are:-

1. Temperature,
2. Rainfall.
3. Type of soil
4. Altitude

Q2. Where are monsoon forests found?

Ans. Monsoon forests are found in South and South East Asia, Central America, Parts of brazil, East Africa and northern Australia.

Q3. Which type of trees are found in the temperate deciduous forest?

Ans. The important species are oak, ash, elm, maple, beech, poplar , redwood and Douglas fir.

Q4. Mention the products obtained from the coniferous forest?

Ans. The yield softwood which is very useful in making furniture, matchstick, paper, newsprint, plywood, sports goods etc.

Q5. What does Tundra vegetation consist of?

Ans. A few stunned trees like willow, birch and alder grow in areas bordering the taiga forest.

Q6. How is deciduous forest different from evergreen forest?

Ans. Evergreen forests are so named as there is no particular season for the trees to shed all their leaves. Therefore, these forests remains green throughout the year. On the other hand, in deciduous forest most of the trees shed their leaves at particular time of the year, usually during the dry season.

Q7. Describe the type of vegetation in Desert?

Ans. Only xerophytic plants, which can adopt themselves to the hot and dry climate, are found here. In the hot desert thorny bushes and shrubs are common . cactus and acacia are the main species. Date palms are found near the oases. Plants here have long roots, thick barks, waxy stems and small leathery leaves to reduce the rate of transpiration. The cold deserts are mostly barren. There are only a few thorny bushes, shrubs and coarse grasses.

Q8. Describe the wildlife of the Tundra region?

Ans. The wildlife of the Tundra region consist of animals which have thick fur or layers of fat to conserve the body heat and enable them to survive in the severe cold. The main land animals found here are reindeer, musk, o, polar bears, dogs, foxes, wolves horse and lemmings in the seas adjoining the coast there are seals, warushes, whales, and different kinds of fish.

Q9. Give an account of the natural vegetation and wildlife of the tropical rainforest?

Ans. The trees are tall with hardwood and broad leaves that form a thick concept at the top. This presents sunlight from penetrating into the forest and the interior are dark and damp. A variety of animals are found such as monkeys, apes, iguanas, pumas, hippopotamuses, crocodile alligators and huge snakes, colourful birds and many insects are found in these forests.

Q10. Describe the location and special features of Mediterranean forests?

Ans. The forests are found in the warm temperature regions on the western margins of continents. In this region summer are dry and rainfall occurs during winters. The forests are not dense and contain broad leaves evergreen trees.

Q11. Compare the tropical and the temperate grasslands under the following heading areas, natural vegetation, wildlife?

Ans. **Tropical grasslands**

- They are located in the tropical latitude in the interior of the continent in the trade wind belt.

- The grass is tall (3m) coarse and spiky which is neither juicy nor nutritive and there are scattered deciduous trees.

- They are known as the 'big game country' as there is a variety of herbivores and carnivores.

- People practice nomadic herding.

- Soil is not very fertile.

- They are known as savannahs in Australia and Africa, and llanos and Campos in S. America.

Temperate Grasslands

- They are located in the temperate latitude in the interior of the continent in the belt of Westernise.

- The grass is short, soft, juicy and nutritive. These are treeless plains as rainfall is less.

- The prairies are known as the 'bread baskets of the world'.

- Commercial farming and commercial herding is carried on.

- Soil is very fertile.

- They are known as prairies in N. America, steppes in Asia, pampas in Argentina and Downs in Australia.

<u>**Grassland Names**</u>

Africa == Savannah

Argentina == Pampa

N. America == Prairies

Australia == Down

Asia & Europe == Steppes

South Africa == Veld

HUMAN ENVIRONMENT

Chapter-12 Human Environment

Fill in the blanks:-

1. **Agriculture** is least likely to be practiced in cities.
2. **USA** has the highest density of road transport in the world.
3. The **Ganga** River in India is a major inland waterway.
4. The Rhone-Rhine canal is located in **Europe.**
5. **Computer** is an example of personal communication.
6. Nomadic people line in **temporary** settlements.
7. In rural settlements the population density is generally **low.**
8. **Waterway** is the cheapest mode of transport.
9. Radio is an example of **mass** communication.

State T/F?

1. Settlements are usually located in areas that have a favorable climates. == **T**
2. The Indian railway commonly use steam engines. == **F**
3. Waterway are the most expensive means of transport. == **F**
4. Fog is great hindrance to the air transport. == **T**

Q1. What do you mean by settlements?

Ans. A settlement is a place where people live and carry out a variety of activities.

Q2. List the factors which govern the development of settlements?

Ans. The factors which govern the development of settlements are favourable climate, availability of land, fertility of soil, water resource, presence of minerals and industries.

Q3. Distinguish between metalled and unmetalled road?

Ans. **Metalled roads:-** they are made up of concrete or asphalt and have a smooth surface. They are all-weather roads and mostly found in towns and cities.

Unmatelled roads:- they are mud roads and have an uneven surface. They are mostly found in rural areas and unfit for use in rainy season.

Q4. Why does Western Europe have one of the dense road and rail network in the world?

Ans. Western Europe have one of the dense road and rail network because there are most heavily industrialized regions of the world with high rate of economic development and a large number of urban centres.

Q5. Mention one advantage and one disadvantage of air transport?

Ans. Air transport is the fastest mean of transport but is very expensive.

Q6. Distinguish between rural and urban settlements?

Ans. **Rural :-** the settlement is one in which majority of people are involved in agriculture and related activites.

Urban :- the settlement in which majority of people are involved in non-agriculture activities. Like, banking, hospital, hotel, and others.

Q7. The development of the transport system depend mainly on the relief features and economic activities of a region. Justify your answer?

Ans. Transport facilitate the movement of goods and people from one place to another. The development of an efficient transport network is essential for the economic prosperity of country.

Q8. What are inland waterway? Give an account of the major inland waterway of the world?

Ans. Inland waterway include river, lakes, canal and steamer which is use to carry passenger and cargo across the inland waterways. Eg.

1. St. Lawrence great lake == North America
2. Rhine == Europe
3. Nile == Africa
4. Ganga- Brahamputra == India

Q9. Explain how rural and urban settlements are complementary to each other?

Ans. Rural and urban settlements are complementary to each other. In rural settlements, majority of the people are engaged in primary activities like agriculture, fishing and mining. The raw materials produced by such primary activities are used in secondary activities in urban areas, such as manufacturing and trading. Villages provide food grains, fruits and vegetables as well as supply of labour force to the cities. The cities, in turn, provide industrial goods needed by the villages.

Q10. Write a short note on the ocean transport?

Ans. Sea routes and oceanic routes are mostly used for transporting merchandise and goods from one country to another. These routes are connected with the ports. Some of the important ports of the world are Singapore and Mumbai in Asia, New York, Los Angeles in North America, Rio de Janerio in South America, Durban and Cape Town in Africa, Sydney in Australia, London and Rotterdam in Europe.

Q11. Write about the various means of communication available to us?

Ans. **Spoken or verbal communication, which includes face-to-face, telephone, radio or television, and other media,** is one of the different types of communication. The telephone or mobile phone is the most popular, modern, and fastest way for two people to exchange information.

LIFE IN TEMERATE REGIONS

<u>Chapter-13 Life in Temperate regions</u>
<u>Fill in the blanks:-</u>

1. Local warm wind in the Prairies is **<u>chinook.</u>**
2. An animal which has been recklessly hunted in the praires is **<u>bison.</u>**
3. The world's biggest meat packing centre is **<u>Chicago.</u>**
4. The ship which yields the finest quality wool is **<u>merino.</u>**
5. **<u>Kimberley</u>** cities in South Africa is famous for its diamond industry.
6. The temperate grassland of South America is called **<u>pampass.</u>**
7. The Canadian prayaries are drained by the **<u>river saskatchewan</u>** and its tributaries.
8. The main workers on the cattle ranch are **<u>cowboy.</u>**
9. The **<u>drakensburg</u>** mountain lie to the southeast of the veld.
10. **<u>Johannesburg</u>** is the largest city in the world.

<u>State T/F?</u>

1. The prairies are located on a plateau. ==F
2. Springbok is an animal found in the prairies. == F
3. The world grasslands have an extreme climate. == F
4. Sheep rearing is more important than cattle rearing in the veld == T
5. The world experience occasional droughts.== T

<u>Q1. What is the location of the praiaries?</u>
Ans. The Prairies in North America located in Canada and the USA.
<u>Q2. Name the rivers that drain the prairies?</u>
Ans. The Mississippi, Missouri, Ohio and Dakota rivers flows through the region while the Canadian prairies are drained by the river Saskatchewan

and its tributaries.

Q3. What is a combine harvester?

Ans. the combine harvester is one modern machine which reaps the crop, threshes, and packs them in in sacks all in one function.

Q4. Why do the prayer is have excellent road and railway network?

Ans. The level and gently sloping land of the Prairies has facilitated the construction of excellent road and railway network.

Q5. What type of wildlife is found in the veld?

Ans. Wildlife in the veld includes Lion, Leopard, Cheetah, Giraffe, Oryx, Springbok etc.

Q6. Why is agriculture in the world not as important as in the prairies?

Ans. Low rainfall, occasional droughts, and poor soil are hindrances to agriculture.

Q7. What makes South Africa a major producer and exporter of wool in the world?

Ans. Sheep rearing is the most important occupation in the veld, South Africa is a major producer and exporter of the wool.

Q8. Name the minerals that are found in the veld region

Ans. The veld is rich in menrals like Gold, Uranium, Diamond, Coal and Iron-ore.

Q9. Compare the climate of Prairies with that of the veld?

Prairies

1. Prairies have extreme climate due to their location in the interior of continent. Both diurnal and annual ranges of temperature are high.

2. Rainfall occurs mostly during spring and summer.

3. Snowfall occurs during winters. Local chinook wind from the Rockies tend to raise temperatures.

Veld

1. Veld has moderate climate owing to higher altitude and proximity to ocean on three sides.

2. Summers are short and rainfall is low with frequent droughts.

3. Winters are long, cool and dry with occasional frost.

Q10. Describe the wildlife of the Prairies?

Ans. The wildlife of Prairies includes wolves, coyotes, jackals, prairies dog, antelopes, rabbits and rattlesnakes. Birds like hawks, owls, and eagles are common.

Q11. Distinguish between animal rearing in the prairies and in the veld?

Ans. Cattle rearing:- The tall and nutritious grasses of the Eastern part of the prairies are very suitable for dairy cattle . Dairy farms produce milk, butter and cheese and are generally located near the big towns. The main occupation of the people of the veld are animal rearing and mining. Cattle rearing is practiced in the warmer and wetter eastern part while sheep are reared in the cooler and drier western part. Dairy products, meat and leather are obtained from cattle. Sheep rearing is very important in the high veld.

Q12. Explain why the Prairies are called " the granary of the world" ?

Ans. The prairies produces huge quantities of wheat, most of which is exported to European and Asian country. This region is thus often referred to as the granary of the world.

Q13. Describe the topography of the veld?

Ans. The veld is located on a plateau descending in a series of steps. The highest part is known as high veld. Its elevation ranges between 1200 m to 1800 m. A ridge called witwatersrand runs through the centre of the high veld. The middle veld ranges in height from 600 m to 1200 m and below it lies the Low veld which ranges from 150m to 600m. The Limpopo, the Sabi, the Orange and its tributary, the vaal, are some of the rivers that drain the veld region. Waterfalls and rapids have formed where the rivers drop down the plateau edges.

LIFE IN HOT AND COLD DESERT

<u>**Chapter- 14 (Life in Hot and Cold Desert)**</u>
<u>**Fill in the blanks:-**</u>

1. The only fresh water lake in Sahara is <u>**Lake Chad.**</u>
2. Willow tree does not grow in Sahara.
3. A tributary of river Indus which flows through <u>**Ladakh is Shyok.**</u>
4. <u>**Zoji La**</u> Mountain pass in Ladakh.
5. An occupation which is not common in Ladakh is <u>**Forestry.**</u>
6. <u>**Emikoussi**</u> is a mountain range in Sahara.
7. The <u>**Tuaregs, Bedounis**</u> are important nomadic tribes in the Sahara.
8. <u>**Sangang**</u> is a huge lake in Ladakh which extends into China.
9. The <u>**Hermis Gompa**</u> is a famous Buddhist manasky in Ladakh.
10. Sedimentary rocks are also called <u>**stratified rocks.**</u>
11. The liberation wild ass is called <u>**Kiang**</u>.

<u>**State T/F?**</u>

1. The Red Sea is located to the north of the Sahara Desert. == <u>**F**</u>
2. The climate of the Sahara is hot and wet. == <u>**T**</u>
3. Cotton is an important commercial crop in the Nile Valley. == <u>**T**</u>
4. Ladakh lies to the north of the Greater Himalayas. == <u>**T**</u>
5. In Ladakh crops are grown in the winter season. == <u>**F**</u>

<u>Q1. What do you understand by a desert?</u>
Ans. Desert is region which receives very low rainfall, has sparse vegetation and extremes of temperature.

Q2. Where is the Sahara Desert located?

Ans. Sahara is the largest desert of the world it is located in northern America.

Q3. Name the crops that grown in the Nile Valley?

Ans. Wheat, maize, millets and Barley.

Q4. Name four cities located in the Sahara?

Ans. Cairo, Giza, Timbuktu, Port said and Alexandria.

Q5. What type of vegetation is found in Ladakh?

Ans. Due to scanty rainfall, the vegetation in Ladakh is sparse. Trees like willow, cypress, elm, juniper and poplar are found there.

Q6. Compare the wildlife of Sahara and the wildlife of Ladakh?

Ans. **Wildlife of Ladakh:-** the wildlife consist of Tibetan antelopes called chiru, wild goats, sheeps, yaks, and Tibetan wild ass called Kiang. Birds like pigeon, carrion, crow, chukar and golden eagle are common in Ladakh.

Wildlife of Sahara:- Desret wildlife consist of antelopes, gazelles, hares, rodents, desert foxes, hyenas, snakes, lizards and different type of insects.

Q7. Bring out the similarities and the differences between agriculture practice in Sahara and Ladakh?

Ans. **In Ladakh agriculture** is practised in the valleys and on the lower slopes crops are grown in summer season from may to September when the temperature is comparatively high wheat Barley vegetables and fruits like apple apricot walnut and grapes are grown in winter the extremely cold weather does not permit agriculture.

In Sahara cultivation of crops is practised in the Nile valley in Egypt and in the oasis serial such as wheat maize Barley and millets are grown date palm is a very valuable tree. Vegetables and fruits like feed olives and apricots are also grown cotton is an important commercial crop in the Nile valley.

Q8. Mention some measures understaken by the government of India to improve the living conditions in Ladakh?

Ans. The Government of India has undertaken a number of measures to improve the living condition of the people of Ladakh transport and communication system is being developed irrigation facilities are being provided the hydropower potential is being trapped and tourism is being promoted on a larger scale.

Q9. Describe the landform features of the Sahara Desert?

Ans. - Sahara is not entirely sandy desert. Their extensive areas of fables and gravel and smooth bare Rocky surfaces the land surface of the Sahara desert does not have uniform relief much of its plane but there are a few plateau and mountain ranges like the range and the agar range Sahara is dotted with several places where water is available then I'll and the major rivers flow along the eastern and the southern borders of that is at respectively lectured is on the southern border is the only freshwater lake in this dessert

Q10. Give an account of animals rearing practiced in the Sahara Desert?

Ans. - The animal herders of the Sahara raise camel sheep and goats. That Tuaregs and the Bedouins are important Nomadic tribes who move from place to place along with their animals in search of water and pictures full stuffed animals provide them milk cow meat and heights. Many of the people of Sahara no longer lead Nomadic life and have now settled down.

Q11. Describe the landform features of Ladakh?

Ans. Ladakh is a cold and Barren desert. There are several mountain passes which provide access to Ladakh. Curriculum and joshila the big ones. The region is drained by the river Indus and its tributaries show just no bra and shuru. These rivers have cut deep valleys in the otherwise Rocky desert surface. There are many glaciers in the region. Pangong so and so Mohini are too big and beautiful lakes in the region.

Q12. Discuss the main occupation of the people of Ladakh?

Ans. Animal rearing agriculture and tourism tourism are the main occupation of the people of Ladakh. Yaks boats and ships are raised on the mountain pictures. It is a very useful animal it provides people with milk own and hear. Sheep and goats are mainly Riyadh for milk meat and own. Full of a very fine quality called pashmina is collected from these gods. Ladakh is famous for producing excellent quality shawls blankets and carpets. Agriculture is practiced in the valleys and on the lower slopes. Crops are grown in summer season from May to September when the temperature is comparatively high.

DEMOCRACY & EQUALITY

Chapter- 15 Democracy & Equality

Ques. A.1: In a democratic country like India equality is at least practised in principle.

ANS.: The statement is true.

Explanation - Equality is the essence of a democratic country like India. The opinions and participation of the people is essential in a democracy. Article 15 of the Indian Constitution prohibits any form of discrimination.Though this is only practised in principle. In reality, inequality among people is prevalent due to various reasons like caste, income and gender.

Ques. A.2: The *Dalits* have been given equal voting rights in India.

ANS.: The statement is true.

Explanation - Dalits exercise the right of universal adult franchise. Every adult citizen, irrespective of his/her caste, colour and creed, is free to vote in India. This ensures equal political rights for all citizens.

Ques. A.3: No minority in India faces discrimination.

ANS.: The statement is false.

Explanation - Discrimination on the basis of caste, colour, creed and gender is prevalent in India. Minorities, for example, the Dalits, are treated unequally. They are deprived of access to services, employment opportunities and education.

Ques. A.4: Midday mean scheme has brought about a social change.

ANS.: The statement is true.

Explanation - The midday meal scheme, launched in 1995, has brought great changes. The number of students has increased and the enrolment of girls has increased. Children of all backgrounds, castes and religion attend schools and have meals together. People from disadvantaged sections of society have found employment as cooks and assistants under this scheme. This has enhanced the speed in bringing social change.

Ques. A.5: <u>America and Europe treat Asians and Blacks with respect.</u>

ANS.: The statement is false.

Explanation - The Asians and Blacks are treated unequally. They are treated like second-class citizens. The disparity does not cease to exist even today, despite abolishment of slavery and granting of equal political rights to Asians and Blacks.

Ques. B.1: <u>Is universal adult franchise important in a democracy? Why?</u>

ANS.: Yes, universal adult franchise is important in a democracy as it is the essence of a democracy. Under the universal adult franchise, the right to vote is given to every adult citizen of a country, irrespective of their colour, caste, creed, gender or education. In a democracy, equality is necessary, which granted by universal adult franchise. It enables the marginalized and weaker sections of society to become stakeholders in choosing representatives who would work for their betterment and thus, underlines a dynamic polity and society.

Ques. B.2: <u>Why, despite the constitutional provision of free education, are all children not able to gain access to education?</u>

ANS.: Free and compulsory education till the age of 14 has been made mandatory by the constitution of India. However, this is not followed in reality. Discrimination on the basis of caste, gender and income is the cause for denial of the right to education. The minorities and dalits are deprived of education. They are made to feel discriminated and are looked down upon by the upper castes. They have not been allowed to go to the same schools as the children of higher class. Many children dropout of schools because of the discrimination they face. Girls are often not sent to school because they are supposed to help in household chores.

Ques. B.3: <u>Why is there prejudice against the minorities in India?</u>

ANS.: In rural India, the grasp of oppression and prejudice against the minorities is high. They generally face discrimination based on their religion, caste and gender. They are denied access to a number of basic needs such as education, equal employment, equal wages and justice. This prejudice against minorities arises as majorities and upper castes see them as outsiders and test their loyalty to their country time and again. It is further accentuated by limited resources in a large population. In such a scenario, community identity takes precedence over individual rights.

Ques. B.4: Read article 15 of the constitution and highlight its main provision on equality?

ANS.: The Article 15 of the constitution focussed upon the prohibition of discrimination on the basis of religion, caste, race, sex or place of birth. This is the main provision of the article. It further emphasises upon the following:

1. No citizen can be deprived of access to restaurants, shops, hotels and public places on grounds of religion, race, caste, sex or place of birth.

2. No citizen can be prohibited from using wells, tanks, bathing ghats, roads and public places maintained by state on discriminatory grounds.

3. The state is not prohibited to make special provisions for women, children and socially backward classes like scheduled castes and scheduled tribes.

Ques. B.5: How has the midday meal served as a means of promoting equality?

ANS.: The mid-day meal scheme, which was initiated on 15th August 1995, has been a means of promoting equality. After the Indian Supreme Court's order on 28th November 2001, government schools have started serving cooked food in all government schools. The enrolment of girls and poor children has risen. Children of both the upper classes and lower classes have the meals together. This reduces the distance between children of different castes. Social changes have also been brought about by this scheme.Women, especially dalit women, and other economically challenged people have been employed as cooks and assistants in the schools. This is an attempt to reduce economic disparity among different sections.

Ques. C.1: Explain with examples the causes of inequality in India.

ANS.: Equality is the essence of a democratic country. However, that is not followed in reality because inequality prevails in India due to various causes. The causes of inequality and their examples are as follows:

1. **Differences in incomes** - Economic inequality seeps through the society because of disparity in income between different sections. For example, the children of rich people get better educational facilities and are enrolled in private schools. The children of poor people are very often not sent to schools at all because of the expenditure.

2. **Discrimination on the basis of castes** - People of the lower caste are treated as untouchables by the upper class people. They are known as dalits and are denied basic rights, further restraining their freedom.

For example, dalits cannot go to temples to offer their prayers. This is a restriction that has been imposed on them by the upper classes. Their children are often also not allowed to go to the same schools where children of the upper class go.

3. **Discrimination on the basis of sex** - Women are denied equal rights as men. The opportunities and benefits granted to men and women are still not equal. For example, a girl is not sent to school because she is supposed to stay at home and do the household chores, whereas a boy of the same age is sent to school and is given an opportunity to earn his living.

Ques. C.2: In what ways are the experiences of African-Americans similar to those of the _Dalits_.

ANS.: The Americans of African origin are treated as second-class citizens and the scheduled castes or dalits of India and are treated as untouchables. The similarities in the experiences of African-Americans and dalits are as follows:

1.The African-Americans have long been treated like slaves by the white majority even after the abolition of slavery Similarly, dalits have been discriminated by the upper classes.

2. Both have been victims of segregation. The blacks or the African-Americans are denied access to clubs, cinemas, parks and other places where the white visits in majority. Dalits are not allowed to visit temples and draw water from the same well as the upper classes do.

3. African-Americans and dalits are not allowed to live in the same neighbourhood as the whites and the upper class, respectively.

4. They are denied access to equal opportunities of education, services and justice.

5. Menial jobs are provided to both African-Americans and dalits.

6. A feeling of insecurity exists among African-Americans and dalits because they consistently face discrimination.

Ques. C.3: Is equality a myth or reality? Present your views.

ANS.: Equality is an ideal, which is practised more in principle. While the idea itself is not a myth, its application certainly is. Several laws and policies have been made to ensure equality and many individuals as well as groups have come together to back this struggle for equality. Inequality happens due to a lot of causes like poverty, religious beliefs and differences in castes. Due to inequality, these backward sections of society are being deprived of education, equal work privileges and basic needs.

Free and compulsory education till the age of 14 is necessary in India. This is not being followed due to discrimination based on caste and gender. The most common example of this discrimination is the social inequality wherein dalits and girls are not allowed to go to schools.

The mid-day meal scheme is one such attempt by the government to motivate poverty-stricken children to come to school for education. It breaks caste barriers as the students, of all castes, upper and lower, can have food under this scheme. It is very effective as apart from provides both nourishment and education to the children, it offers employment opportunities to the people of the society in the form of cooks and caretakers.

The disparities have already seeped through the social and economic strata of the country. Although the Article 15 of the Indian Constitution promotes the prevention of such discrimination, it would take time to materialise in reality.

INSTITUTION OF DEMOCRACY

Chapter-16 Institution of Democracy

Q1. List any two social groups who were denied voting rights initially in most democratic countries?

Ans. Women, Poor and Black people group.

Q2. What is the role of an opposition party?

Ans. The opposition party, they criticize the policies of the government forcing the government to work for the welfare of the people.

Q3. What is an electronic voting machine?

Ans. The process of voting is simplified with the electronic voting machine.

Q4. Name two major type of political parties and give one example of each?

Ans. 1. National party à Congress, BJP (Bharatiya Janata Party)

2. Regional party à Siromani Akali Dal, Punjab.

Q5. What is ballet paper?

Ans. People used to caste their vote by putting a stamp on ballet paper.

Q6. Why are the elections important in democracy?

Ans. The elections are important in democracy because:-

- Elections are the means of expression of public will.
- By electing candidates of their choice, people participate in the government of their country.
- Elections held at regular interval give the people a choice to allow the present government rule for a longer time or elect new government.
- A free and fair election offers real choice of the people.

Q7. State the importance of universal adult franchise?

Ans. The importance of UAF:-

- UAF shows political equality.
- It encourages young people to participate in the election process.
- It initiates people in the act of choosing their representative.
- It brings the power a government based on the consent of the power.

Q8. What does the election commission plays in the election process?

Ans. The task of holding election in the country is exhausted to an independent constitutional body called election commission. The election commission undertake the responsibility of conducting free and fair election t regular intervals. The election commission has the right to allow symbols to the political parties. It gives recognition to the national parties, state parties and regional parties. It sets limits on poll expenses. The commission prepare electoral rolls and update the voter's list from time to time.

Q9. Distinguish between national and regional party?

Ans. **National Party:**

a. A party that secures at least 6% of total votes in the Lok Sabha elections or Assembly elections in four states and wins at least 2 seats is recognized as a national party.

b. These parties raise issues of national importance.

c. Example: INC, BJP, BSP, CPI-M, CPI, NCP and AITC.

Regional Party:

a. A party that secures at least 6% of total votes in an election to the Legislative Assembly of a state and wins at least 4 seats is recognized as a regional party/state party.

b. These parties raise issues of regional importance.

c. Example: Samajwadi Party, Rashtriya Janata Dal, DMK, AIADMK, etc.

Q10. Why do we need symbols for every political party?

Ans. we need symbols for every political party So that even the illiterate people are able to recognize the political party on the basis of their symbols. The illiterate people are not able to read and write and hence they find difficulty to read the political party's name but symbols help them to make it easy to recognize a political party

Fill in the blanks:-

1. The universal adult franchise was accepted in United States of America in the year **1965.**
2. People who fight elections on their own and without the support of political parties are called **independent candidate.**
3. A government formed with the alliance of two or more parties is called **coalition government.**
4. **AIADMK** is a regional party of Tamil nadu.
5. The constitution of India grants the right to vote to all Indian citizen of and above the age of **18 years.**
6. Individual who contest an election without belonging to any party is called **independent candidate.**
7. A national party is one that contest election from at least **four** states.
8. The **opposing** party criticize the policies of the government forcing the government to work for the welfare of the people.
9. The head of the election commission of India is the chief election commissioner who is appointed by the **president**.
10. Party symbol are approved by the **election commission**.

STATE GOVERNMENT

Chapter-17 State government
Fill in the blanks:-

1. The member of the **legislative assembly** elect the speaker and deputy speaker from among them.
2. Person who can be elected to the legislative assembly should **be citizen of India.**
3. The chief minister and his council of ministers run the state administration in the name of **the governor.**
4. The strength of the legislative consul should not be more than **one- third** the size of the legislative assembly of that state.
5. To be a governor a person must **be the citizen of India.**
6. The **legislative council** elects the chairman and a deputy chairman from among them to preside over the working of the council.
7. A proposal for a laws is termed **as a bill.**
8. The unicameral state legislature has only one house which is **legislative assembly.**
9. **The money bill** can be introduced only in the legislative assembly.
10. The **legislative council** is a permanent body and cannot be dissolved.

State true or False.

1. State government make the policies for the entire country. ==F
2. The council of minister in a state consist of the chief minister and the minister appointed by him. == T
3. The legislative assembly is a permanent house that cannot be dissolved. ==F
4. The legislative council passes the money bill. ==F

5. The most populous state Mizoram has 400 members in the legislative assembly. == F

Ques1. How many state and union territories does the India have?
Ans. 28 states and 9 union territories.

Ques2. What are the organs of the state government?
Ans. The state government comprises three organ executive legislator and judiciary.

Ques3. What is the term of the legislative assembly?
Ans. The term of legislative assembly is 5 years.

Ques4. How many type of Bella there name them?
Ans. A proposal for a law is termed as a bill there are two type of will money bill and non money bill.

Ques5. Who appoints the governor?
Ans. President appoints the governor.

Ques6. What are the qualifications of a governor?
Ans. To be a governor a person must full fill the following conditions:-

1. They should be a citizen of India
2. They must not be less than 35 years of age.
3. They must not be a member of either of the two houses of parliament or of the state legislature.
4. They must not hold any government office.

Ques7. How are the powers of the state government different from the powers of the union government?
Ans. **The powers of the state government** are mentioned in the state list. The subjects on which the state government can make laws are maintaining law and order in the state, health, police, land policies, transport etc. **The powers of the union government** are mentioned in the union list. The subjects on which the union government can make laws are of national importance. These are railways, currency, external affairs, defence, banking, post and telegraph, etc.

Ques8. How does a bill become a law?
Ans. Once the bill is discuss in approved by the houses it is sent to the governor for their signature after the governor's signature the bill becomes a law.

<u>Ques9. Who appoints the governor of a state how long does he remain in the power?</u>

Ans. The governor is appointed by the president for the term of 5 years however the president may removed them from office before the completion of the term.

<u>Ques10. When can a governor dissolve the assembly before it completed term?</u>

Ans. When a **government** is unable to prove its **majority** and also when a 'No-confidence motion' is passed then a **governor can dissolve the assembly.**

Ques11. Bring out the difference between legislative assembly and legislative council?

Legislative Assembly

1. Legislative Assembly is the lower house of the State legislature, whose members represents the people of the State, as they are directly elected by the people.
2. Temporary body (LA)
3. Direct election.(LA)
4. Maximum members are 500, while minimum members are 60. (LA)
5. Minimum age for Membership 25 years (LA)
6. Presiding Officer Speaker (LA)

Legislative Council

1. Legislative Council is the upper house of Indian States, which follows a bicameral legislature, whose members are partly elected and partly nominated.
2. Permanent Body (LC)
3. Indirect Election (LC)
4. One third of the total members of VidhanSabha, but it should not be less than 40. (LC)
5. Minimum age for Membership 30 years (LC)
6. Presiding Chairmen

Ques12. Discuss the power and function of legislative assembly?

Ans. The legislative assembly has mainly two type of functions- Legislative and financial

Legislative powers assembly is empowered to make the law pertaining to the subject mention in the state list and the concurrent list of the constitution.

Financial power the assembly enjoys supreme authority with respect to the passing of the state budget, money bill, permission to laying taxes, and fixing salaries of the member of state legislature.

Ques13. Which of the two house of the state legislature is more powerful? Why?

Ans. The Legislative Assembly or the Vidhan Sabha is the powerful House of thie state legislature its members are elected by the people. All important decisions and policies are made by this House Money Bills can only be introduced here, it also controls the executives.

Ques14. What are the special powers that are exercised by your governor?

The powers of Governor of a state are :-

1. The Governor appoints the leader of the majority party or the coalition as the Chief Minister.
2. All appointments to high offices in the state are made by the Governor.
3. He can address, summon and dissolve the Legislative Assembly.
4. The Governor can reduce or pardon the punishment awarded to a criminal under the state rules.
5. Every bill, which the State Legislative Assembly passes, becomes a law only after the consent of the Governor.

Ques15. How is the chief minister appointed? Discuss their main function?

Ans."Chief Minister" is appointed by the "nominal executive head" of the state or "Governor". He is the "real executive" and "principal head" of the state. He is the "communicative channel" between the "Governor" and "council of ministers". Governor appointed the ministers who are recommended by the "Chief Minister", so he Coordinates, controls and allocates portfolios to the "council of ministers". If Chief Minister died during his tenure, total council of ministers are dissolved.

WORKING OF STATE GOVERNMENT

Chapter-18 Working of State Government
Fill in the blanks:-

1. The state has the responsibility to ensure that citizen are provided with **Proper healthcare , education , employment.**
2. The infrastructure at the healthcare centres includes **medicines**
3. The sector in healthcare which has better facilities is the **private sector**
4. The private healthcare sector is driven by **welfare goals**
5. The private healthcare services are **Expensive** and can not be afforded by everybody.
6. A **Healthy** person is physically fit and free of illness.
7. Health is **Human** for all the people .
8. Public healthcare centres take care of health in the **Urban and rural**

   areas.

   9. The **private** states that providing health facility is the primary
responsibility of the government .

10. Gender discrimination is a factor which **Universal** access to healthcare facilities.

State whether true or false .

1. Health is a matter of human rights and its violation should be seen as a violation of human rights. ==F
2. The state of Kerala was formed in the year 1957. ==F

3. The national health mission defines health as a state of complete physical, mental and social well-being and not merely an absence of disease or infirmity. ==T
4. The private health services are profit oriented and hence expensive. ==T
5. The district hospitals supervise the rural health centres. ==T

Q1. What do you understand by health?
Ans:- Health means our ability to remain free of illness and injuries.

Q2. what are public health facilities?
Ans:- public health facilities take care of health in the urban and rural areas.

Q3. What does the court uphold as one of the primary responsibilities of government?
Ans:- The court has upheld that providing healthcare services to the general public is the primary responsibility of government.

Q4. Which sections of society experience inequality in healthcare facilities?
Ans:- Healthcare facilities are not readily available to all sections of the society.

Q5. Write about the three tier structure that exists in public health services?
Ans:- The primary health care infrastructure has been developed as a three tier system with sub centre , primary health centre (CHC) being the three pillars of primary health care. system.

Q6. Why are the poor unable to receive proper medical attention?
Ans:- Poor are unable to access health care because they are able to afford money for the health care, moreover they are educated to understand the importance of health , our government should take steps and create awareness to the poor people about the importance of healthcare.

Q7. List some disadvantages of public health services?
Ans:- The following are some of the drawbacks of our healthcare-

- Most doctors settle in urban areas, fewer doctors in rural areas.
- Two million cases of malaria and five lakh cases of tuberculosis every year.
- Water-borne communicable diseases like diarrhoea, hepatitis on the rise.
- Half of all children are malnourished.

GENDER & GENDER INEQUALITY

<u>Chapter-19 Gender and gender inequality</u>
<u>Fill in the blanks:-</u>

1. Women are mostly seen as a **<u>homemaker.</u>**
2. The widow remarriage act was passed in 1856 with the efforts **<u>of Ishwar Chand Vidyasagar</u>**.
3. The government has made it mandatory for any organization to make an arrangement for child care service if it has more than **<u>60</u>** women employees.
4. After independence our **<u>constitution</u>** granted equal rights to men and women in all sphere of life.
5. **<u>Sati</u>** is an inhuman practice under which married women burn herself at the pyre of her husband after his death.
6. Gender roles have created **<u>disparity.</u>**
7. Dayanand Saraswati emphasize on **<u>girl child education.</u>**
8. The house hold work that women do is **<u>under value.</u>**
9. **<u>Gender inequality</u>** is the differential treatment of the two sex resulting the preference of one sex over the other.
10. About **<u>75% of</u>** the jobs in the well paid professions are held by men.

<u>State T/ F?</u>

1. Our society is based on equality, hence there is no discrimination between men and women. ==**<u>F</u>**
2. Defining gender roles leads to gender inequality. ==**<u>T</u>**
3. Gender inequality in India is a recent phenomenon. ==**<u>F</u>**

4. Women work outside home is appreciated. == **F**
5. When resources are limited parents prefer to send boys to school rather than girls. == **T**

Q1. What do you understand by gender?

Ans The social construct of roles, responsibilities and norms that are based on biological differences between a boy and a girl is referred to as gender. Gender thus is a construct of the society.

Q2. List two gender stereotypes that you usually come across?

Ans. A few stereotypes that we witness around us are as follows:

1. Boys do not cry.
2. Girls are really bad in mathematics.
3. Girls are bad drivers.
4. Boys are really good at playing video games and adapting to technology.

Q3. What do understand by gender inequality?

Ans. Gender inequality can be understood as the inequality in status of men and women in the society. It has existed in the Indian society since ages and its root lays in the biological differences between a boy and a girl. This inequality is manifested in several forms, mainly in the form of roles and expectations.

Q4. Distinguish between gender and sex?

Ans. The term sex refers to the biological differences between males and females, such as genitalia and genetic differences. Gender is more difficult to define it can refer to the role of a male and female in the society , known as gender role, or gender identity.

Q5. Why do you think there is inequality in jobs for men and women?

Ans. Inequality in jobs for men and women is witnessed in the Indian society. For a very long time, women have been considered best suited for taking care of family and as a homemaker. They are not supposed to go out and work but, rather they are expected to stay in the house and look after their husband, children and family. Also, this household service is free of cost as they are not even paid for it. The economic value of service rendered is not accounted.

Women still are not regarded suitable for strenuous or office work. Still believed to be meek and feeble, serves as the ground for all inequalities.

Q6. Housework is meant for women. Do you agree? Support your answer?

Ans. In the Indian society, a woman is seen as a housewife, cook, mother, sister and a daughter who is given the responsibility to take care of her family, husband and children. She is given a lower status in society as compared to her male counterpart. A woman is also expected to be good at handling family affairs and not go out of her house for any other work. She is not even paid anything for doing all the household tasks rather she is also expected to stay economically dependent. In my opinion, a woman is equally good in all aspects of life, be it family or office. She can effectively handle all the pressure that comes with managing family with office work. She must be given equal opportunity for her own growth, which will, in turn, help in the development of society all together. A man should not engage himself only in office, he should also participate in the household work to better appreciate the challenges faced by a woman and move towards equal division of work. This would also enable him to appreciate the dignity and importance of all kinds of work.

Q7. What measures has the government taken to abolish the gender inequality?

Ans. the measures that govt has taken are as follows-

(1)Several programs have been launched by the government to promote girls education like **beti bachao beti padhao.**

(2) Hindi dowry laws has been implemented.

(3) history laws have been made against domestic violence.

(4) female infanticide and sex selective abortion have been declared illegal.

(5) the equal remuneration act 1976 have been implemented so that men and women are equal wages for equal work.

(6) one third seats are reserved for women in Panchayat and municipalities.

Q8. Discuss the impact of gender inequality can have on people?

Ans. Structural gender inequalities in the allocation of resources, such as income, education, health care, nutrition and political voice, are strongly associated with poor health and reduced well-being. Very often, such structural gender discrimination of women in many other areas has an indirect impact on women's health.

Q9. Name a few social reformers who worked for the upliftment of women. Also mention the reforms introduced by them.

1. **Raja Ram Mohan Roy** à abolishment of evil practice of Sati in the year 1829.
2. **Ishwar Chand Vidyasagar** à Widow Remarriage Act in the year 1856.
3. **Dayanand Saraswati** à opened several schools for girl child and he played an important role in the field of women's education

1. **Raja Ram Mohan Roy** à abolishment of evil practice of Sati in the year 1829.
2. **Ishwar Chand Vidyasagar** à Widow Remarriage Act in the year 1856.

HEALTHCARE IN STATE GOVERNMENT

Chapter- 20 Healthcare in State Government.
Fill in the blanks:-

1. The state has the responsibility to ensure that citizens are provided with **proper healthcare.**
2. The infrastructure at the healthcare centers includes **medicines.**
3. The sector to healthcare which has better facilities is the **public sector.**
4. The private healthcare sector is driven by **profits.**
5. The private healthcare services are **expensive** and cannot be afforded by everybody.
6. A **healthy** person is physically fit and free of illness.
7. Health is **fundamental right** for all the people.
8. Public healthcare centres take care of health in the **rural** areas.
9. The **constituted** state that providing health facility is the primary responsibility of the government.
10. Gender discrimination is a factor which **denies** access to healthcare.

State T/F?

1. Health is a matter of human rights and its violation should be seen as a violation of human rights. == T
2. The state of Kerala was formed in the year 1957. == F
3. The National Health Mission defines health as a state of complete physical, mental and social well-being and not merely an absence of disease or infirmity. == T
4. The private health service are profit oriented and hence expensive. = T

5.   The district hospitals supervise the rural health centres. == T

Q1. What do you understand by health?
Ans. Health is a state of physical and mental well being.
Q2. What are public health facilities?
Ans. Providing health and basic facilities to the people is a primary responsibility of any government.
Q3. What does the court uphold as one of the primary responsibility of government?
Ans. Judiciary upholds the spirit of constitution and regards it as the primary responsibility of the government too.
Q4. Which section of society experiences inequality in healthcare facilities?
Ans. Women also face inequality in health services. Often the health of women is considered less important than the male members of the family.
Q5. Write about three tier structure that exists in public health service?
Ans. The three tiers of the Medical system level ---
1. Primary Health Care System:
It is also called basic medical care in India. For example-
Sub center
PHC center
2. Secondary health system:
This level acts as the first referral unit or FRU of the healthcare system. For example –
Community Health Center or CHC
County Hospital
3. Three tier health system
The supreme medical tier of the Indian healthcare unit. For example - -
Regional hospital
Super specialty hospital
Medical hospital
Q7. Why are the poor enable to receive proper medical attention?
Ans. People in remote area with little transport facilities cannot dream of being prompt medical treatment in times of illness. There is not only a paucity of doctors and nurses in such remote areas. But also travelling vast distances to reach a healthcare centre is not possible for many poor people.
Q8. List some disadvantages of public health service?

Ans. The disadvantages of public health service are poor, lack of ownership of health and limitation of free medicines program.

Q9. Compare private and public healthcare facilities?

Private Health Care

1. Private health facilities are not owned or controlled by the government.

2. Better and faster service is available but very expensive.

3. They are well equipped with modern machines and technologies

4. Only rich people with good earnings can afford this service

Public Health Care

1. The public health service is a chain of health centres and hospitals run by the government.

2. Comparatively cheaper, delay in service due to over-crowding of people

3. Lack of proper equipment and technologies

4. Available at a cheaper cost for everyone

Q10. Discuss the ways in which government can provide healthcare to all?

Ans. The government can take necessary steps to provide healthcare for all by:

- Increasing the amount of hospitals, healthcare centres, and family welfare centres.
- Organising free camps for the check-up of the overall public.
- Organising Pulse Polio campaigns.
- Spreading health awareness among folk through different means. Workshops, seminars, and training camps also can prove to be effective ways.
- To provide healthcare for all, the govt can provide appropriate facilities such as laboratories for testing, ambulance services, blood banks etc. additionally to this,resources like doctors, nurses, technicians also as equipment need to be properly channeled.